A WISH YOU WERE HERE BOOK ®

YELLOWSTONE

BY JIM WILSON, LYNN WILSON & JEFF NICHOLAS

ACKNOWLEDGEMENTS

We wish to thank Gene Ball, Tim Manns (North District Naturalist), and the National Park Service and its employees, both past and present. It is due to their foresight and hard work that such wonderlands as Yellowstone are still here for each of us to enjoy. It is up to each of us, as individuals, to make certain our own use is consistent with the long-term needs of these natural temples.

This book is dedicated
to those who stop:

to see, to hear, to smell, to taste, to feel,

not just to know,
but to understand.

P. O. Box 25, El Portal, Ca. 95318
ISBN 0-939365-08-1
Printed in Hong Kong

INTRODUCTION

From our many travels we feel smaller and smaller in the overwhelming diversity of Mother Nature. Each encounter is more than just the visual aspect of the moment, but becomes a total sensory experience. Yellowstone captivated our attention with its unique "windows" into the heart of our planet, delighted us with its wildlife, filled our beings with incredible smells and music, elevated color and texture to a higher plane and renewed our inner spirit with its sedate tranquility. Each time we enter into one of Mother Nature's "magic kingdoms" we are reminded that she is the ultimate teacher. At the proper time she prepares the meadow, uses fire to cleanse the land and arranges the seasons to replenish moisture. We have found

that all things are a complement to each other and incomplete when element is absent. To this end we encourage a respectful appreciation of Yellowstone National Park-- an example of Mother Nature at her finest.

Lynn Jim Jeff

YELLOWSTONE

BY JIM WILSON, LYNN WILSON & JEFF NICHOLAS

I wish you were here, for this is a land of music:
from the heavens filled with the osprey's cry
to the bugling of elk-filled meadows;
from the splashing of sun-dappled fish
to the explosive eruption of Old Faithful.

Bull Elk, Sunset Fog

Riverside Geyser

These geothermal features, "windows" into the heart of Mother Earth, entice the intellect to explore the inner workings of this planet and reflect on Man's relationship to his surroundings. These sights, sounds, smells and textures stimulate the senses to a new plateau of enjoyment.

Hot Spring, West Thumb

Slowly the Earth liberates a deep, thunderous groan and the hot, muggy air smells of sulphur. Dormant vents awaken with hissing steam, spewing forth bursts of water. A repetitive thumping echoes from an enormous submerged cavity.................. The sleeping giant erupts in a rare flash of glory.

Daisy Geyser

Old Faithful, Winter Sunset

Old Faithful, Sunrise

The ground quakes,
the boardwalks roll
and an explosion of water
fills the heavens.
Billowing clouds of steam
erupt higher and higher,
lavishing the fortunate
few with a warm,
ancient mist.

Old Faithful, Winter Explosion

Clepsydra Geyser, Sunset

The heat of day fades into twilight and the earth's pools are transformed into mirrors reflecting the setting sun's last glow. The night sky softens the land with the brightness of its stars. Summer breezes sing through Lodgepole Pines, harmonizing with the scurryings of nocturnal life. Moonlight, solitude, and Old Faithful fill the soul with peace and serenity; there is nothing as stirring as silent moonbeams passing through a spewing geyser.

Pork Chop Geyser and Big Dipper

Jupiter Spring, Winter

Like a vanilla sundae covered with extravagant toppings, the Mammoth Terraces unite travertine with brilliant algae to form what appears to be a delicately glazed dessert. Songbirds preen their feathers in these warm, trickling pools, splashing about in a palatial bath. Pronghorns shyly graze the hills above, ambling from one browse to the next.

Minerva Terrace

Canary Spring

One hears a resounding CRACK. Then another. Two Bighorn rams ritualistically butt their massive foreheads together vying for the loyalty of the harem. Raising their noses, baring their teeth, they slam into one another with a fierce intensity. One's entire attention is captivated with their grace and fortitude. It is even said by some that "time spent in the presence of Bighorns does not count against your life-span".

Bighorn Ram

Norris Geyser Basin, Winter

Like a multicolored mosaic, iridescent hot springs abound where the earth's crust is thinnest. The most torrid pools radiate a rich aquamarine, and are so clear one can see deep into their bottomless pits. The intense volume of steam and lack of light occasionally veil their impenetrable depths.

Morning Glory Pool

Grand Prismatic Spring

These pools are scalloped with ornate edges of finely textured geyserite, deposited layer by layer for thousands of years. Warm waters laden with rainbow-colored algae cascade into the shallow waters.

Doublet Pool

Lower Yellowstone Falls From Artists Point

At twilight the gorge of the Grand Canyon of the Yellowstone glows in a pastel palette of rock and sand. Along the rim the wind whistles through the trees, steam is seen rising from the ridges far below and the claws of squirrels click as they scurry across the scree. Prankster ravens glide above the canyon depths mocking those who are bound to earth.

Yellowstone River From Inspiration Point

Tower Fall

Water abounds in this land of heat and steam. Whether in the serenity of a glassy lake at sunrise or in the exhilaration of watching a river suddenly drop off a ledge and plunge to a churning pool,water holds a unique fascination for most people.

Sunrise Above Virginia Cascades

Wildflower Display

Spring hillsides are dazzling
tapestries of fresh flowers.
Droning bees,
hovering hummingbirds
and colorful butterflies share
in Nature's fragrant ambrosia.
Basking marmots chirp at
passersby and grizzlies roam
through fields of blossoms.

Grizzly, Sage and Blossoms

Clockwise: Pronghorn, Elk, Bison, Moose Calf

Fecund meadows smell musty with the advent of spring. Newborn elk, buffalo and moose frolic in the nursery of Mother Nature. Free of the womb, little elk kick their heels and chase butterflies in a wild garden. Young moose give pursuit to reticent water fowl, awkwardly splashing about. Youthful buffalo play "stampede", running in and out of the adult herd. Meanwhile, mothers all continue to feed, patiently ignoring such youthful frivolity.

Trumpeter Swan

Bull Moose, Sunrise

In the early light of dawn the "fishermen" appear. Graceful pelicans soar the motionless waters of Yellowstone Lake, their black tipped feathers rippling the glassy surface. Carried on currents known only to them, ospreys circle marshy shorelines. Keen eyes send these swift birds into a power dive. A solitary fly fisherman casts his line into a foggy, waist-deep river, whipping line and feather across a calm section of water.

Clockwise: Osprey, Cutthroat Trout, Fly Fisherman, White Pelican

Grizzly In Autumn Grass

All who enter Yellowstone pass through the shadow of the grizzly. Although rarely seen, his powerful presence overwhelms any event. One is aware, when walking through this wilderness that the grizzly is lord of this land. Just the thought of his existence evokes an almost unbearable excitement. It is sufficient just to know that he is here.......Free.

Solitary Conifer in Snow

Bison, First Snow

Golden grass sways in the breeze, reflecting the setting sun. As Summer winds down buffalo suitors begin their mating rituals. Guttural grunts and friendly nuzzling excite the female to engage in courtship.

The chill of evening marks the approach of Autumn. A virile elk lifts his massive rack and bugles. Another answers. Soon the noise of male superiority echoes throughout the valley, and so falls the first flake of snow.

Bull Elk, Winter

Ghost Tree, Shoshone Geyser Basin

Snow covers the meadows and the land takes on new contours. White flocked pines melt in geyser steam, while the sub-zero temperature refreezes the moisture into stunning ice sculptures. These crystalline branched trees glisten prismatically against an azure sky.

Middle Geyser Basin, Winter

Winter Sunrise, Upper Geyser Basin

The warming sun, the exhilaration of a good ski, an erupting geyser's steam turning to ice crystals before reaching the surrounding snow, the glow of a pine-scented fire, the smell of soup and homemade bread ---- all make up Winter.

Winter Sunset, Lamar Valley

Sunset, Porcelain Basin

I wish you were
here, for this is a
land of music: from
the heavens filled
with the osprey's cry
to the bugling of
elk-filled meadows;
from the splashing
of sun-dappled fish
to the explosive
eruption of
Old Faithful.

Bull Moose, Autumn Fog

Hot Spring, Yellowstone Lake

Look into these "windows" of Mother Earth and know her pulse. Experience the inner workings of this planet and reflect on man's relationship to it, for Nature's heartbeat dictates the future of mankind.

White Dome Geyser

NOTES ON THE PHOTOGRAPHS

Cover: Great Fountain Geyser, Sunset.

Title Page: Bison, Yellowstone Lake, Winter. The bison *(Bison bison)* is the largest land mammal on the North American continent; bulls can weigh 2000 pounds or more. The species was hunted to near extinction in the late nineteenth century motivated by human greed. With the creation of Yellowstone National Park, a haven was ultimately created for what is now the world's largest herd of American Bison.

5. Bull Elk, Sunset Fog. Each Autumn, elk bulls *(Cervus canadensis)* gather their harems of 6 to 30 cows. The rutting season begins with a bull's ritual bugling. Throughout the mating season bulls chase off less aggressive males and occasionally engage in battle to establish their dominance.

6. Riverside Geyser. This geyser is located on the Firehole River in the Upper Geyser Basin. Its 75-foot eruption lasts approximately twenty minutes, arching gracefully into the river.

7. Hot Spring, West Thumb. Though not the largest or most popular, the West Thumb Geyser Basin should not be overlooked. Its collection of pools and hot springs are among the most impressive and colorful in the Park.

8. Daisy Geyser. Daisy is another of the major geysers located in the Upper Geyser Basin. It is quite regular and usually predictable. The angular eruption will reach 75 feet and, for the unsuspecting, will provide a warm mineral shower.

9. Old Faithful, Winter Sunset. To most visitors Old Faithful *is* Yellowstone. It has become, a worldwide symbol of this great Park. While it is neither the highest nor the most regular of geysers, it is accessible and consistent, and an awesome sight to first time visitors.

10. Old Faithful, Sunrise. The geysers in Upper Geyser Basin are fueled almost exclusively by surface water, rain and snowmelt seeping through cracks in the bedrock and superheated by the hot rocks below. During a typical eruption Old Faithful will spew up to 7500 gallons of water into the atmosphere.

11. Old Faithful, Winter Explosion. Combine sub- zero winter temperatures with 204° F. water and Old Faithful's 100 to over 180-foot eruption appears to be three times higher. This enormous plume of steam, often resembling a mushroom cloud, will quickly convince any skeptic that this is a magnificent geological event.

12. Clepsydra Geyser, Sunset. This highly active geyser is located at the Fountain Paint Pots. Its eruption rarely ceases. Combined with a low western horizon, Clepsydra provides photographers with a spectacular sunset.

13. Pork Chop Geyser and Big Dipper. Moonlight and twinkling stars reveal a soft, romantic vision of Yellowstone's mighty geysers. Even the most popular will continue to erupt unobserved under this most spectacular lighting of all.

14. Jupiter Spring, Winter. During extreme winter temperatures minute airborne crystals often form a thick blanket of fog obscuring the sun throughout daylight hours. Here at Jupiter Spring only the dead tree trunks rise above the snow.

15. Minerva Terrace. The ornate terraces formed by Minerva Spring are a center of attraction for all those who visit Mammoth Hot Springs. Unlike other thermal features in the Park, these formations change dramatically, often depositing up to 8 inches of travertine each year.

16. Canary Spring. Located in the Upper Terrace, this exceptionally colorful formation is the multi-jeweled crown of Mammoth Hot Springs. Varying temperature zones in the water channels paint ribbons of algal color.

17. Bighorn Ram. The shy bighorn sheep*(Ovis canadensis)* are a magnificent sight and are found in only a few locations in the Park. During the summer months they can usually be seen in the upper elevations around Mt. Washburn. They once were an important food source for Yellowstone's only year round human inhabitants, the primitive Sheepeater Indians.

18. Norris Geyser Basin, Winter. The Norris Geyser Basin is a thermal area deserving of superlatives: the world's highest geyser (Steamboat) and the Park's hottest exposed area (Porcelain Basin) are but two of the noted features. A visit here also provides an opportunity to see the reliable Echinus Geyser.

19. Morning Glory Pool. Shaped as its botanical namesake implies, reflections of the azure sky make this pool an impressive sight. Due in part to seismic activity and in part to visitors depositing coins and debris, this pool is a classic example of being "loved to death". After a period of cloudiness as a result of the debris, the now protected Morning Glory Pool is beginning to regain some of its former glory.

20. Grand Prismatic Spring. When conditions are right, Grand Prismatic Spring, the largest in Yellowstone, displays the most stunning palette of saturated color imaginable. The streaks and swirls of color are attributed to various types of algae growing in the shallow runoff apron.

21. Doublet Pool. Ornately scalloped edges of pastel siliceous sinter and ominous dark water give this twin-lobed pool a forbidding, prehistoric appearance. Doublet Pool is on Geyser Hill overlooking Old Faithful Inn.

22. Lower Yellowstone Falls From Artists Point. The Yellowstone River flows through a deep canyon of soft, hydrothermally altered rhyolitic lava. In two locations along the water course are intrusions of harder, less altered, rhyolites which form spectacular waterfalls. The upper fall is 109 feet while the lower plunges 308 feet.

23. Yellowstone River From Inspiration Point. The steep, angular walls in the Grand Canyon of the Yellowstone converge 800 to 1200 feet below the rim to form the course of the outflow of Yellowstone Lake. The pastel yellow and orange-hued walls were deposited by the Canyon Rhyolite flow 590,000 years ago.

24. Tower Fall. Yellowstone is a land of water and, as one would expect, a land of many waterfalls. Some are readily accessible and others require some hiking. The 132-foot Tower Fall is easily seen from near the road but the best view is at the end of a short trail which descends to its base.

25. Sunrise Above Virginia Cascades. The upper reaches of the Gibbon River is an idyllic setting for a picnic or a relaxing afternoon. The river opens up into a broad grassy meadow which is rarely visited, a great place to escape the summer crowds.

26. Wildflower Display. Spring comes late to this high Rocky Mountain wildflower garden. The open hillsides around Dunraven Pass display rainbows of blossoms, usually from late June to mid-August.

27. Grizzly, Sage and Blossoms. *(Ursus horribilis)* The Yellowstone area offers one of the best chances of survival for this magnificent threatened species in the lower 48 states. Their voracious appetite for plants, nuts, berries, ants, rodents, fish, insects and other animals requires a vast area of wilderness to support a population.

28. Wildlife. The Yellowstone area offers the visitor an opportunity to view more large wild animal species than in any other area of North America. Clockwise: pronghorn (Antilocapra americana); bison (Bison bison); elk cow and calf (Cervus canadensis); moose calf (Alces alces).

29. Trumpeter Swan. This rare and graceful waterfowl has found this park to its liking. Several widely scattered areas provide sanctuary and breeding grounds. These elegant white birds are easily recognized by their long graceful necks.

30. Bull Moose, Sunrise. The moose (Alces alces) is the largest and most impressive of the ungulates that live in Yellowstone. It stands up to six feet tall and can weigh up to 1200 pounds. During Summer and Fall they can be found widely scattered along the Lewis River, Hayden Valley, Lower Pelican Creek and Willow Park.

31. Fishermen. Fishing, whether by bird, mammal or humans, is an important activity inside Yellowstone National Park. Clockwise: osprey in flight; cutthroat trout; fly fisherman at sunrise; white pelicans in Yellowstone Lake.

32. Grizzly In Autumn Grass. During the Fall, grizzlies prepare for the long cold winter to come. Their preferred food this time of year is the Whitebark Pine nut. Grizzlies will dig a den or seek out a cave and drift into a long sleep from November to March. Their metabolism consequently slows down and they will exist only on stored body fat accumulated during Fall feedings.

33.Solitary Conifer in Snow. The harsh winter season of the Greater Yellowstone Area often becomes Nature's tool for controlling wildlife population. For those species who remain, the deep snow pack and extreme temperatures cause stress and physical hardship making it difficult for the weak to survive. The struggle for life can be traced by the network of tracks left in the snow.

34. Bison, First Snow. During winter, many bison migrate to the thermal areas. The warmth offers both a sanctuary from bitter cold and accessible browsing for available forage. When snow deepens, they use their broad foreheads to bulldoze a furrow down to the food supply.

35. Bull Elk, Winter. The world's largest concentration of Rocky Mountain Elk can be found within the Park. Weighing 600 to 1000 pounds, the males wear a heavy, branching crown of antlers which will be shed in late winter.

36. Ghost Tree, Shoshone Geyser Basin. Moist steam rising from thermal areas collects on tree limbs only to freeze, producing a delicate lacework of prismatic branches.

37. Middle Geyser Basin. The season's first snowfall brings a stunning blanket of simplicity to the landscape. Hidden from view are the meadows, rocks and wood litered forest floors. Only the warm waters of the geysers and hot springs can carve a clear pathway through the thick winter mantle.

38. Winter Sunrise, Upper Geyser Basin. The Firehole River flows through this basin on its way to joining the

Madison River. Each day during the long cold Winter it is the willing recipient of millions of gallons of warm mineral water from erupting geysers.

39. Winter Sunset, Lamar Valley. This long broad valley was glacially carved during the last Ice Age, ending 10,000 years ago. Today the Lamar River meanders through this area, creating open grass and sageland which supports large numbers of mammals and waterfowl.

40. Sunset, Porcelain Basin. Norris Geyser Basin is divided by a low east-west ridge. To the south is the Back Basin featuring, among others, Steamboat and Echinus Geysers. To the north is Porcelain Basin, whose broad flat bottom provides the ideal environment for many varieties of algae, each one a different hue, swirling and blending to create pastel rainbows.

41. Bull Moose, Autumn Fog. The primary diet of the nearly 1000 moose in the Park consists of submerged roots, water lilies, willow and other twigs and leaves. These ungulates rarely eat grasses. Only the males grow antlers but both sexes develop a growth of skin and fur, called the bell, which hangs from the neck.

42. Hot Spring, Yellowstone Lake. The islands of this country's largest high elevation lake provide sanctuaries for large numbers of Yellowston's bird population. Frank Island features many osprey nests while the Molly Islands are a protected breeding ground for the White Pelicans.

43. White Dome Geyser. This geyser is located eight miles north of Old Faithful on the Firehole Lake Drive. Its 7 to 45-foot eruptions last approximately two minutes and occur three or more times per hour.

PHOTO CREDITS:

Jim Wilson: 6, 7, 8, 9, 10, 15, 16, 19, 20, 21, 23, 24, 25, 28b, 34, 40, 42, 48
Jeff Nicholas: 14, 18, 28c, 33, 37
Dewitt Jones: Front Cover
Jeff Henry: Title Page, 11 ,27, 31b, 31c, 31d, 32, 38, 41
Diana Stratton: 5, 12, 26, 28a, 28d, 29
Lewis Kemper: 22, 30, 39
Jeffrey Hogan: 17, 35
Steve Nelson: 13, 43
Jeff Cobb: 36
John Stevens: 31a

Virginia Cascades Road, Autumn 1988